by David

For Sharon

PRODUCTION NOTES

The play is written tightly and demands fast tight playing. Although clothing changes between scenes are needed these can be minimal as Claire would tend to wear the "power" suits of the time and Adrian would wear his "uniform" too. Keep the audience driven along. Adrian's only major change is into "tramp" clothes for his final entrance, for which he has plenty of time.

Adrian is forceful and confident when in work and boyishly enthusiastic when planning. He swings into depression easily and has a soft side. Claire is a forceful scheming women, quite capable of anything to achieve her ends. She should develop the hardness as the play progresses to contrast with her false femininity with Campbell and her lovey dovey exchange with Allan, and to provide the believable platform for the final act. Handle that final part carefully - it could make or break the entire performance.

CAST

ADRIAN . . . . . *Typical Yuppie of the 80s, enthusiastic, driving*

CLAIRE . . . . *His wife, an attractive but hard woman*

ALLAN . . . . *Their friend*

KEITH . . . . *Similar in build to Adrian - a drop out*

SGT CAMPBELL

WPC JOHNSON

Scene 1

The scene is a smart high-tech living room of the late 80's. There is a door US to the hall, and window Stage R. It is early evening. We hear the sound of the outside door opening, and then being closed loudly. ADRIAN appears, jacket slung over his shoulder, wearing braces and tie. He has been drinking.

ADRIAN: Hello, hello. Anybody there? Light of my life, sweet passion flower, where are you? *(goes back into hall, calls up stairs)* Are you up there dearest? Are you waiting for me with bated breath and skimpy nightie? No? In the kitchen perhaps! *(he disappears for a moment)* - no. Not in there either. Never around when you want her. *(He flings down his briefcase, and loosens his tie, tosses jacket on back of chair)* So, welcome home Adrian. How are you dear? What sort of day have you had? Oh! Oh dear! That's terrible. Come and sit down, I'll get you a drink *(he gets bottle and sits)* Now tell me all about it. There you go.

Is that enough? No, better have a spot more. You look pretty shattered. There. *(takes large gulp)* That's better. Bitch! I need you. Just for once in your self centred life you might have been here! *(another drink)* But no. I'll bet it's another client. The clients must come first. Huh! *(the outside door is heard to open and close again)* Ah! The wanderer returns. *(he puts his feet up on the coffee table)* Is that you dear?

(Claire appears, dressed smartly in "office" suit.)

CLAIRE: Hi there. Sorry I'm a bit late. I got stuck with a client... oh for heaven's sake Adrian! Can't I leave you on your own for five minutes? Look at you!

ADRIAN: Hello darling. What sort of day have you had at the office? Oh, not very good actually...

CLAIRE: Do you have to take to the bottle at the least excuse? Look at you! Sit up and get your feet off the furniture.

ADRIAN: Yes Mother. *(he sits up)*

CLAIRE: You're pathetic. Why couldn't you have made yourself something to eat? There's plenty in the fridge. I bet you haven't eaten all day.

ADRIAN: Lunch is for wimps!

CLAIRE: Lunch, in your case, helps sop up the alcohol. Right. We better get some food in you I suppose.

ADRIAN: Hang on Claire. Don't you want to know what's happened?

CLAIRE: Save it till after the food.

ADRIAN: Sit down, sit down. Food can wait. Do you know what happened today?

CLAIRE: *(sits, with a sigh)* Okay, tell me, but don't spin it out like you usually do. I could do with a bite to eat too. Don't tell me old Hugh's got one over on you.

ADRIAN: Ha! That'll be the day. This is a lot worse than Hugh.

CLAIRE: It must be bad.

ADRIAN: It is. It's redundancy.

CLAIRE: They're making you redundant? But I thought...

ADRIAN: Not just me - all of us. The whole gang. Out on our ears. Smith Markinson are going bust. Down the tubes. They are an ex-company.

CLAIRE: But you need your job - they can't be going bust! It's only three weeks since you were saying how well you had done. That big deal you pulled off. You reckoned Hugh would be out...

ADRIAN: Well, I got that bit right. Didn't think I'd be joining him though.

CLAIRE: What about notice and...

ADRIAN: Oh, I've no doubt we will get official notice, once it's definite.

CLAIRE: Once it's definite? You mean it isn't?

ADRIAN: They're not making it official - yet.

CLAIRE: Well, that's not so bad.

ADRIAN: Not so bad! That's like saying you're slightly pregnant.

CLAIRE: So if it's not official, who's saying it's going to happen?

ADRIAN: The markets. It's all over everywhere. Take it from me, good old SM is on the skids. They've overextended their capital. That and a couple of deals that didn't work out the way they should have. *(pause)* God knows if I'll get anything! If they go bust - actually bust - we might get nothing.

CLAIRE: What about another job?

ADRIAN: There's a general cutback everywhere at the moment.

CLAIRE: What happened to "make it happen "? You reckon that's your life slogan: "There's them that watch things happen, them that things happen to, and then there's them that *make it happen*". You're always going on about it. So, you say it's only a rumour, get on the phone, use those contacts you're always going on about. Somebody somewhere...

ADRIAN: They're all hanging onto what they've got.

CLAIRE: Get on the phone! Make it happen.

ADRIAN: I'll do it tomorrow.

CLAIRE: It's better to get in while it's still a rumour than after the event. At this moment 60 SM employees are busy telling their other halves the same story you've just told me. They are all saying - the employees' other halves - "Oh you poor dear. How terrible for you. Never mind. Maybe it won't come to anything". Like a bunch of ostriches they ignore everything until it reaches up and smacks them in the face.

ADRIAN: Some of that supportive stuff was what...

CLAIRE: Cuddles and coos are fine for after the event, but not when there are things that can be done. Those 60 staff...

ADRIAN: 59.

CLAIRE: Okay, 59. There's no need to be exact.

ADRIAN: I was merely anticipating the fact that I will be the one to act differently.

CLAIRE: Right. That is exactly my point. All those staff will have been comforted and lulled into a false sense of security. You, on the other hand, will get in first.

ADRIAN: Boldly going where no man has gone before?

CLAIRE: I hate you when you get to this stage.

ADRIAN: Does that mean that momma isn't going to sooth poppa's fevered brow?

CLAIRE: I'm more likely to put a dent in it if you don't get serious! There are times Adrian when I could strangle you.

ADRIAN: Okay, okay. *(gets mobile phone and filofax from jacket)* I shall begin Operation Jobhunt. Hey! Why don't I pop down the Bull? There are usually a few of the guys in there...

CLAIRE: Phone!

ADRIAN: Face to face is better for this kind of thing.

CLAIRE: If you go to the Bull you won't remember who you've talked to, never mind whether they offered you a job. *(crosses and picks up bottle)* I'm going to make something to eat. You won't need this in the meantime. I'll leave the door open, so I expect to hear constructive conversation. *(she exits)*

ADRIAN: *(opening filofax)* "Constructive conversation." Huh! *(thought. He pretends to dial.)* Hello, hello, is that you Mr Leggo..? Yes, it's Adrian, the boy wonder.... how's tricks? Or should that be how's bricks? *(laughs, Claire reappears.)*

CLAIRE: Grow up Adrian. This is not a funny situation.

(She exits)

ADRIAN: *(resigned, consults filofax and dials)* Hello Chaz? It's Ad... oh you've heard...? You don't have any little spaces over there for a fine young.... yes, yes, I quite understand.... No, it's not a major prob, just thought I'd ......yeh, see you, ciao.

LIGHTS FADE as he consults filofax and dials another number.

Scene 2

The same, two weeks later. Evening. Claire is in the room. Similar business suit, without the jacket.

CLAIRE: *(the outside door opens and closes)* Hello! Is that you Adrian?

ADRIAN: *(appearing with wet overcoat over his arm)* Who else were you expecting? The neighbourhood stud?

CLAIRE: That's charming - how did you get soaked? Did your car break down?

ADRIAN: I have no car. I have no car because they took the keys away this afternoon, just after they handed out the official redundancy notices. *(He dumps his coat and goes to get drink)* Well, at least I can't be done for drink driving... *(pulls out envelope)* One official redundancy notice.

CLAIRE: So, it's confirmed. I thought that since it has been two weeks since you heard the rumours...

ADRIAN: They've done well to hang on this long.

CLAIRE: So when do you finish up?

ADRIAN: I have. Within half an hour of getting this. Off the premises. Security apparently. Didn't want us screwing them even further into the red. *(sits)* So that's it. I can now consider myself retired.

CLAIRE: Have you still not managed to get anything?

ADRIAN: Look Claire. I have called in every favour I was owed. I've made dozens of calls. I've even tried complete strangers. Oh! There's a great shortage of double-glazing salesmen - or I could try my hand at being a security guard, but I have no intention of doing either! I've still got some professional pride.

CLAIRE: Is your professional pride going to pay the bills?

ADRIAN: We don't get any bills we can avoid. Strictly basics from now on. Food - nothing fancy - gas, electricity, phone - I'll get shot of my mobile - mortgage. That's about it. Do you realise quite the mess we are in?

CLAIRE: It can't be all that bad. We've got the house and...

ADRIAN: Correction. The building society has the house. We just pay the mortgage, and God knows how we keep that up on your salary. Maybe we could move somewhere smaller for the short term, rent a...

CLAIRE: We can't sell this place! We wouldn't get the money to pay off the loan. We'd be short about £50,000 - and then there's all the fees...

ADRIAN: Great! So we're stuck with a house that's worth less than the loan we took out on it. Thanks to you.

CLAIRE: How do you make it my fault?

ADRIAN: It was your idea to go for the maximum. "It'll be a good investment" you said. "Bricks and mortar never let you down" you said.

CLAIRE: At the time...

ADRIAN: At the time, we bought for £120,000 with a 95% loan. What do you reckon it's worth now?

CLAIRE: £70-75,000 I suppose.

ADRIAN: So we can't sell. And we won't manage to keep the payments up for long. I suppose they'll repossess...

CLAIRE: It's not my fault!

ADRIAN: I trusted your professional judgement Miss Estate Agent. *(downs drink and goes for refill)* Well, from now on, I'll rely on my own.

CLAIRE: Yes, you do that. Great track record that has. Out on your ear without a warning when you're supposed to be an investment expert...

ADRIAN: Commodities dearest, not business.

CLAIRE: Same difference.

ADRIAN: It's not! Listen...

CLAIRE: Who cares? Commodities, business, you didn't see it coming, and now we're going to lose all this.

ADRIAN: We'll survive. What a mess! *(drinks)*

CLAIRE: That's one thing that can go. The drink. It's a non-essential. And from now on, since it's my money that'll keep us going, I'll decide what's essential.

ADRIAN: We'll see about that.

CLAIRE: Right. Now that you've got that out of your system I'm going out. I had hoped to have a quick bite but I haven't time now.

ADRIAN: You've only just got here! You're always working late these days. I thought the market was slow?

CLAIRE: The market is slow, so I have to work when any opportunity presents itself. It's my job, and I - we are going to need that job. See you later.

ADRIAN: Oh hell! You know what?

CLAIRE: *(stops at door and turns)* What now?

ADRIAN: I'd be better off dead.

CLAIRE: Don't talk stupid. Get a grip on yourself.

ADRIAN: No, it's true. We were discussing it in the pub at lunchtime. If I dropped dead here and now, all our problems would be solved.

CLAIRE: *(easing into room)* How do you make that out?

ADRIAN: Life assurance. I get four times my annual salary if I snuff it while employed by good old SM.

CLAIRE: But they've just made you redundant.

ADRIAN: I'm still on their books until the period of notice runs out. That's twelve weeks. We stand to make enough to clear the mortgage. Well, you'd stand to make it. I'd be lying down, because I'd be dead. You're not laughing. That was a joke.

CLAIRE: It wasn't funny Adrian. Anyway, you're not likely to drop dead, unless it's from liver failure, so just stick to practicalities.

ADRIAN: All I would need to do is find a way to "die" and still come back to collect. There's been films and...

CLAIRE: Fiction, not fact.

ADRIAN: "Make it Happen". Remember? If I put my mind to it...

CLAIRE: Your first priority is to find work. I've got to go. I'm going to be late.

ADRIAN: Off you go. By the time you come back I'll have worked something out.

CLAIRE: That's highly unlikely. *(she goes)*

ADRIAN: I'll show you! Right, the problem is: I have to appear to die but still be able to collect on the insurance, so that means - disappearance? Possibly. Now, let's get a piece of paper - *(he goes for briefcase as LIGHTS FADE. Pause. When lights come back he is deep in planning . We hear the front door. CLAIRE enters.)*

ADRIAN: Hi. I've worked out some ideas on this false death...

CLAIRE: You should be concentrating on finding work.

ADRIAN: I've done that. Read the book, bought the T shirt, watched the video. Anyway, where the hell have you been till this time of night?

CLAIRE: Doing my job.

ADRIAN: It takes three hours to show someone over a house?

CLAIRE: It takes time to get there and back as well - and, if you are that interested, it was actually three calls. I thought they were interested in the second one, so I took them back for another look.

ADRIAN: Fine. I'm going to need to spend some time in the Library - looking up some details.

CLAIRE: You're wasting time Adrian. It's been tried, but never succeeded.

ADRIAN: How do you know it hasn't? If it had succeeded then you wouldn't know, would you? That's the whole point. It's like the perfect murder.

CLAIRE: And just as non-existent. These sort of things only happen in books. Why don't you just admit defeat? The big problem is the mortgage...

ADRIAN: Thanks to you.

CLAIRE: We're back on that are we? It's all my fault. What about approaching the building society? See if they'd agree to some sort of deal.

ADRIAN: They probably would, but only in the short term. We might get a few months' leeway. *(pause)* I wish we had a coal fire. You could see things in a coal fire. It helped you think.

CLAIRE: I'm beginning to worry about you Adrian.

ADRIAN: Hang on. I think I've got it! We've been stuck with the idea of me having to "die" - you know, we need to have my body. But we don't need a body, do we? You can be presumed dead, can't you?

CLAIRE: Yes, but it takes quite a while for the legal process. I mean, look at Lord Lucan...

ADRIAN: Yes, well, he killed somebody, so it's a bit different.

CLAIRE: You can't go around presuming someone's dead just because they disappear for a few days. We've had cases where houses have lain empty for years and we can't sell them because the owner has disappeared...

ADRIAN: I suppose you're right. Never mind. I'll think of something.

CLAIRE: Right. I suppose I might as well clear up and get to bed. I suppose you'll just sit there and drink yourself silly...

ADRIAN: I haven't had a drink since you went out!

CLAIRE: Good for you. So, are you coming to bed?

ADRIAN: Not just yet. I can't sleep.

CLAIRE: Then go to the Doctor tomorrow and get something to help you sleep.

ADRIAN: I don't like taking pills.

CLAIRE: Then go for a walk, or have a hot bath, drink a mug of cocoa. Anything. But just lay off the booze. We can't afford it, as you said about other things.

ADRIAN: Would you like to - just once - try to help instead of knocking me back all the time?

CLAIRE: I'm just being realistic. All right. Just for the moment, let's presume that you have found a way to feign death, and you've come back. What then? You can't come back as yourself.

ADRIAN: I'd get a new identity. Like Edward Fox did in Day of the Jackal.

CLAIRE: So what are you going to do in this new identity - to make money?

ADRIAN: My hotel. I've always figured on retiring early and buying a hotel.

CLAIRE: How are you going to afford that?

ADRIAN: That's where the bonus comes in. I've worked it out. *(finds papers)* See? I get four times my salary...

CLAIRE: Which clears the mortgage.

ADRIAN: No. That's the bonus! You see, the mortgage is an endowment, so...

CLAIRE: ...the policy takes care of the loan if you die! I hadn't though of that.

ADRIAN: You see? I thought it out, you know. So the lump sum is clear profit. Enough to buy a reasonable place - not round here - I reckon Norwich would be...

CLAIRE: Norwich! That's Outer Mongolia! It's dead. it's...

ADRIAN: It's where we've never been. Somewhere I know nobody and nobody knows me.

CLAIRE: You expect me to move away from here, from all our friends...

ADRIAN: We have to. I can't be dead one minute and then reappear. After the funeral you sell up and move. No forwarding address.

CLAIRE: You make it all sound too easy.

ADRIAN: It is easy.

CLAIRE: Maybe. And you're sure that Smith Markinson will have the money to pay up?

ADRIAN: No problem. It's guaranteed even if they are completely bust.

CLAIRE: It does seem to have possibilities.

ADRIAN: That bit's easy. It's the first part that's the difficult bit.

CLAIRE: You could fall off a Channel Ferry...

ADRIAN: And how am I going to survive?

CLAIRE: You needn't fall overboard. You could hide in a lifeboat. I'd say you fell. I could say you had been depressed...

ADRIAN: No! Not on any account. If you say that it's suicide they won't pay out.

CLAIRE: Oh. A fire! Your body would be burnt to ashes.

ADRIAN: Still be bones though. Maybe you've got something though *(pause)* You might not like this. It's a bit gruesome. If we burnt somebody else's body, out of all recognition...

CLAIRE: And who are you going to get to volunteer for the burnt offering? Anyway, wouldn't they still do checks?

ADRIAN: Not if you were there and positively identified the remains. They'd have no reason to check. They'd take your word for it. After all, why should you lie?

CLAIRE: What about the body? "You" need to be found burnt. How do we find a body?

ADRIAN: That does need some thought, but...

CLAIRE: *(had enough)* You should be thinking about getting a job. That's the important thing.

ADRIAN: I can't get a job! The probability of me getting a job before this notice period runs out is about 0.1% So, if that's the only avenue I explore, we'll end up in cardboard city. Along with all the rest of the flotsam and jetsam of society.

CLAIRE: That's it! Cardboard city. That's where you'll find a body. It's full of people who could disappear without anyone worrying.

ADRIAN: You mean find a dropout...

CLAIRE: Desperate situations call for desperate remedies Adrian. Let's see. We get him interested by offering him a bath and a meal, some fresh clothes. Get him back here. Put some sleeping pills in his drink. You go to the Doc tomorrow and get some. When he's asleep - burn the body, like you said.

ADRIAN: Where? In the garden?

CLAIRE: You'll have to take him somewhere. Got it! Henry's boat!

ADRIAN: That old heap that he goes fishing in?

CLAIRE: He said you could use it any time you wanted. Give him a buzz when we've found a suitable drop out - and that'll be that. All you need to do is arrange a leak on the old gas heater he uses in the cabin. Hey presto, big fire and boat sinks.

ADRIAN: It'll need some thinking out...

CLAIRE: Come on. Get your coat on. No time like the present. It's getting late. They'll be settling down.

ADRIAN: Who?

CLAIRE: The drop outs - in cardboard city. *(she ushers him out)*

   LIGHTS FADE

Scene 3

The same. Several days later. CLAIRE, ADRIAN and KEITH are seated. Keith is similar to Adrian in build, his hair a little damp - he's just had a bath. He wears clothes of Adrian's.

ADRIAN: So, anyway, *(look at Claire)* how are you feeling now Keith? You must be tired - I mean, what with a big meal and your soak in the bath. Maybe you'd like a lie down?

CLAIRE: For heaven's sake Adrian! Leave the man alone. *(with emphasis)* When he's sleepy, he'll let us know.

ADRIAN: Yes, sorry *(pause)*

CLAIRE: Just ignore him Keith. That's what I always do.

KEITH: When do I get this hundred quid?

ADRIAN: Tomorrow Keith, tomorrow. No need to worry about that now.

KEITH: Should be a start. I might be able to get digs. If I get an address the Benefit might be willing - I used to have money. You never have enough though, do you?

CLAIRE: Would you like another drink?

KEITH: Oh, yeah! No. Better not. If I start hitting the sauce too much - Pity. It's good stuff this too.

ADRIAN: I'm glad you appreciate it.

KEITH: Well I wasn't always a bum.

CLAIRE: Of course not! And that's what this is all about Keith. We give you a chance to make it back...

KEITH: You must find it difficult doing this...

ADRIAN: Difficult?

KEITH: You want to be careful. Some of the guys can be real nasty. There's druggies and all sorts - *(he yawns)* You be careful. A nice looking woman like you...

CLAIRE: Thank you.

KEITH: Well, just be warned. That's all. *(he's getting sleepy)* A hundred quid! Sounds a lot, but - God I'm tired!

ADRIAN: It's the food and...

KEITH: Look, this might be a good idea. A bit of mutual aid. You want to watch out for that too - Aids.

CLAIRE: I think it might be better to tell us tomorrow...

KEITH: You've got a big place here - more than enough room. Why don't I stick around for a while? I could help you pick out the right people, and with a decent kip and food...

CLAIRE: *(sharply)* No, Keith. This is strictly overnight.

KEITH: But I could do some odd jobs. I'm quite handy...

CLAIRE: No! The deal is as we said. Bed and breakfast and then Adrian runs you wherever you want to go...

KEITH: Yeah, I get the message. *(He slumps back, half asleep.)*

ADRIAN: *(pulling Claire downstage)* Maybe we should listen to what he...

CLAIRE: Maybe nothing. We stick to the plan.

ADRIAN: I've been thinking about this...

CLAIRE: You haven't changed your mind have you!

ADRIAN: Ssh! *(pulling her further away from Keith)* We don't want him to hear. He's nearly asleep.

CLAIRE: About time too. He's nodded off now. How much longer should we wait? *(checks)* He's out for the count now. So what are you waiting for? Get him out into the car.

ADRIAN: That's what I want to have a word about.

CLAIRE: What now? You've got someone - a nobody that nobody is going to miss. We've bathed him, wined and dined him, and stuck him in some of your clothes.

ADRIAN: All that bit is fine

CLAIRE: It should be! It's taken us four days to come up with someone that fits the bill!

ADRIAN: Yes, but...

CLAIRE: You haven't forgotten to ask Henry about his boat?

ADRIAN: Of course not...

CLAIRE: Right. So get on with it. Get him out into the boot of the car and off you go. It'll take you over an hour to get there.

ADRIAN: Well, that's what I was thinking about...

CLAIRE: All right, all right. I'll come with you. I suppose I can stand on the quay and wave you off out to sea. And I'll be able to make sure you don't drive like an idiot. The last thing you want is the Police stopping you.

ADRIAN: Do you think we gave him enough sleeping pills?

CLAIRE: What's this "we"? I left that to you. Can't you do anything right?

ADRIAN: I didn't want to use too many...

CLAIRE: Why not? What difference would it make?

ADRIAN: Well, just in case they check. They might find it a bit strange if he was chocablock with sleeping pills.

CLAIRE: The whole idea is that they wouldn't check.

ADRIAN: He's actually not too bad now that he's cleaned up. He seems like he might make a go of it. I've been thinking about this...

CLAIRE: You're not going soft on me...

ADRIAN: It's not a question of going soft. There's just a helluva difference between talking about it and actually doing it.

CLAIRE: God Almighty! You don't have to do "it". He's sound asleep. Where's the problem?

ADRIAN: It's the actual - killing.

CLAIRE: He's oblivious to it all. All you do is set fire to the boat...

ADRIAN: What if he wakes up?

CLAIRE: He's sound asleep.

ADRIAN: Maybe I could hit him with something before - you know.

CLAIRE: Are you mad? You can't do that! The Police are going to notice a great big dent in his skull!

ADRIAN: But you don't realise...

CLAIRE: I realise that you're chickening out!

ADRIAN: We don't know how long the pills will keep him out.

CLAIRE: Tie him up! Gag him! There are times Adrian when I wonder...

ADRIAN: But that means I'd have to untie him before I set fire to the boat. He'd be conscious when the fire starts.

CLAIRE: *(misunderstanding)* Of course! If he yelled out, someone might hear.

ADRIAN: It was OK when we worked it out. Clinical. I can't go through with it now. Not, not after sitting at the table with him. He's quite a nice bloke really. Just had a rough break. What happened with his wife was...

CLAIRE: I hadn't thought about the noise - Maybe...

ADRIAN: I've made up my mind. Tomorrow I run him to a hostel or wherever...

CLAIRE: Think of the money! We need that money.

ADRIAN: I can't do it Claire!

CLAIRE: God, what a wimp! All talk and no trousers - that's always been your problem.

ADRIAN: Just ask yourself Claire: would you sleep easy for the rest of your life? Or would you be stuck with the memory of his screams as he burnt to death? I'd never sleep again. No. Keith goes back, safe and sound. Maybe one day he'll amount to something, thanks to us.

CLAIRE: Great! We're about to end up on the streets and you turn do-gooder! Right, I'll do it myself. *(She attempts to lift Keith)* Damn! Damn, damn, damn! *(She sits)* Right. Have it your way Adrian. Take your friend back where he came from. *(shouting)* Now, Adrian. And you can stay with him for all I care. Get out! Go on! You're worse than useless! You belong with the drop outs, so get going.

ADRIAN: *(a long look at Claire)* I worry about you Claire... *(a glare from her)* All right. I'm going. *(he gets Keith up in a fireman's lift and struggles out with him. We hear the outer door open and close.)*

CLAIRE: *(Rises, looks out through curtains, then she takes mobile phone from her handbag. She closes door, and dials.)* Hello, I hope I didn't disturb you... *(laughs)* You have that effect on me too... no, it hasn't worked. He's chickened out... he's taking him back to the arches... well I thought I had him convinced, I thought he'd go through with it... we've tried it that way, so I'll just have to think of another way... that sounds very interesting, but physically impossible Allan... *(giggles)* Now, be serious.....but I want him to suffer, whatever happens, he has to suffer..... we'll talk about it at lunch....usual time....See you then Allan, Night, night darling.

(she shuts off phone and stands looking pleased with herself as LIGHTS FADE)

Scene 4

The same. The next morning. Claire is in housecoat, looking worried. She is on the phone.

CLAIRE: But I can't help being worried Allan! He's not come back, and it's after seven now.........I need you Allan, can't you come over, please?......do you think I should phone the Police?.........there are times when I wish you weren't a solicitor Allan. You always have to consider everything before........you will? Oh thank you darling. You are a treasure. You don't know how much this means to me. I'm at my wits' end......no, I won't do anything. I'll wait for you. Be as quick as you can. *(she puts phone down. Stands and thinks for a minute, then goes out to kitchen. The door bell rings. She crosses back to front door.)*

CAMPBELL: *(off)* Mrs Claire Thorpe? I wonder if we might have a word. I'm Detective Sergeant Campbell, and this is WPC Johnson.

CLAIRE: Police! What's happened? Has Adrian had an accident?

CAMPBELL: It might be better if we came in Mrs Thorpe.

CLAIRE: Yes, yes, of course. *(She appears with DS CAMPBELL and WPC JOHNSON.)* So what's happened? My husband's been out all night, he...

CAMPBELL: Why don't you sit down Mrs Thorpe? *(she does)* I'm afraid we have rather bad news for you. Mrs Thorpe, are you the owner of a white Ford XR2. registration mark F 713..?

CLAIRE: That's my car! What's happened?

CAMPBELL: We found your car on some waste ground back of West Street, about an hour ago. One of our patrols spotted it.

CLAIRE: Is it damaged?

CAMPBELL: I'm afraid so, Mrs Thorpe. It's not unusual in these cases. It's been burnt out I'm afraid. You mentioned that your husband...

CLAIRE: He went out last night and hasn't came back. I've been worried about him, trying to make up my mind whether to phone you - the Police...

CAMPBELL: Was your husband driving the car?

CLAIRE: Yes. Yes, he was. *(pause as they wait for her enquiry)*

CAMPBELL: Was your husband alone in the car Mrs Thorpe?

CLAIRE: Yes, he was. Well, no, actually he wasn't. He had someone with him.

CAMPBELL: Just one passenger? Might I ask who that was?

CLAIRE: It was - look Sergeant - do you mind if I take a moment to put something on? It's rather cold...

CAMPBELL: Not at all, not at all. And WPC Johnson might slip the kettle on - if you don't mind?

CLAIRE: Right. (She gathers up phone as she goes.)

CAMPBELL: A cup of Rosie's tea will soon warm you up. Won't it Rosie?

WPC: I do my best, Sarge. (She goes off with Claire. Campbell has a look round the room. WPC comes back on.) Kettle's on.

CAMPBELL: Nice house. Bit Spartan for my taste though.

WPC: It's all the latest. High-tech. They're obviously doing well.

CAMPBELL: Yes. When we started asking about who her husband had with him in the car, she got very edgy.

WPC: You reckon the getting dressed thing was just to give her time to think?

CAMPBELL: Probably to contact someone. She took the phone with her.

WPC: Maybe I should let her know the tea's ready?

CAMPBELL: You read my mind Rosie. Quietly though.

WPC: Like a mouse, Sarge. (she goes off)

CAMPBELL: (Sampling a chair and laying his gloves down beside it) So what was hubby up to in your car that you'd rather we didn't know about Mrs Thorpe? Why not his own car? And what was he doing down West Street way? Hardly the sort of district for his type of upwardly mobile young executive to be. I wonder if they're into drugs? I'm told it's quite the thing in smart circles. (Claire enters on this last line)

CLAIRE: What's quite the thing Sergeant?

CAMPBELL: Ah there you are Mrs Thorpe. Rosie will be in with the tea in a minute.

CLAIRE: You were saying...

CAMPBELL: Sorry about that. Bad habit of mine - talking to myself. I was just remarking on the decor. Very fashionable I believe.

CLAIRE: We try to keep up.

CAMPBELL: Mrs Campbell and I are a bit more traditional. Old fashioned you would probably call it. *(Rosie cames in with three mugs.)*

WPC: Here we are! Sorry about the mugs, but you don't want to trust the Sarge with fine china.

CAMPBELL: Ah, that's better. Now. You were telling me about the person who went of in your car with your husband. When was this? Last night?

CLAIRE: Yes, last night.

CAMPBELL: Was this a business friend of Mr Thorpe's?

CLAIRE: Well, no. My husband is being made redundant Sergeant, and he thought up this scheme to occupy himself, and help others.

CAMPBELL: Go on.

CLAIRE: He was helping down and outs make a fresh start.

CAMPBELL: A worthy cause - in some cases. Was he working with one of the registered charities?

CLAIRE: No. It was just him. He found a - suitable - person, we gave him a bath and a square meal and a bed for the night.

WPC: It would take more than that to reform most of the ones I've come across.

CLAIRE: Yes, well, Adrian also gave them some money - not a lot, but enough to maybe get them some digs for a few days.

(Campbell and Johnson exchange looks)

Well he thought he was doing some good!

CAMPBELL: Perhaps he was. Perhaps he was. Tell me this though. If you washed and fed the homeless and gave them a warm bed, why was Mr Thorpe taking this one back?

CLAIRE: The man got quite greedy. He wanted more money. He wanted to stay over for a while. So Adrian decided he'd better get him back.

CAMPBELL: Did he turn violent?

CLAIRE: No, nothing like that. He was just - a bit unwilling to accept the offer we made. He went with Adrian without a fuss.

CAMPBELL: And this was about?

CLAIRE: Oh, about half past ten, maybe a bit later.

CAMPBELL: What was his name?

CLAIRE: His name?

CAMPBELL: Even the homeless have names.

CLAIRE: Yes, of course, it was - Jim.

CAMPBELL: Jim - what?

CLAIRE: Just Jim. Adrian didn't think we needed to know too much about - you know.

CAMPBELL: So your husband drove off at 10.30 with a man he hardly knew to go back into an area the Police tend to avoid. Did he have any money?

CLAIRE: Adrian? Of course - he had the £100 he had promised the man. Sergeant, are you saying that something has...

CAMPBELL: We found someone in the car. Well, to be blunt, the remains of someone, because it was a pretty fierce fire. Deliberate. No doubt about that. We can't be sure at this stage Mrs Thorpe. The fire has made it very difficult to identify...

CLAIRE: It's Adrian! I know it's Adrian! The fool! I told him it wasn't safe going down amongst those people.

CAMPBELL: You gave him good advice Mrs Thorpe. We have very little at this stage, but one thing you could help us with...

CLAIRE: Of course. The man - Jim - was about 40, quite thin, about 5 foot seven or thereabouts. Not very tall. He had dark brown hair. Long.

CAMPBELL: Thank you for that. But what I wanted to say...

CLAIRE: Adrian picked him up down at the arches, he said. I think that's quite near where you found the car.

WPC: Yes, it is. I think Sergeant Campbell was...

CLAIRE: Was he killed before the car was set on fire?

(they look at her) I'd hate to think of him suffering.

WPC: *(with look at Sergeant)* I think you can take it that he was not aware of the fire Mrs Thorpe. Jim, or some of his friends, probably attacked him for the money he had, and then decided to burn the car to destroy any evidence. But, as I was saying, you could help us...

CLAIRE: Anything. Anything I can do to help.

CAMPBELL: Do you know what your husband was wearing?

CLAIRE: Wearing? I thought you said it was all burnt?

CAMPBELL: Sorry. Let me be a little more specific. Did your husband wear cufflinks?

CLAIRE: Yes, he did. Always. *(realisation)* It's his Ancient Order of Froth Blowers.

CAMPBELL: Pardon?

CLAIRE: AOFB. An old fashioned pair of chain links with AO on the one and FB on the other. He got them from his Dad. Always wore them.

CAMPBELL: *(reaching in pocket)* Are these the ones?

CLAIRE: Yes, yes! They're Adrian's. You found them...

WPC: In the car.

CLAIRE: Oh Adrian! Adrian! *(she weeps copiously)*

WPC: I'm sorry Mrs Thorpe. Look, have you anyone who can come in and be with you?

CLAIRE: My Mum and Dad. I'll ring them...

CAMPBELL: Weren't they in then?

CLAIRE: Sorry?

CAMPBELL: I noticed you take the phone with you when you went up to change.

CLAIRE: Oh, yes, of course. How observant of you. No, there was no answer. Probably out with the dog.

WPC: Why not try them again now?

CLAIRE: Right, I will. *(She gets phone out and dials.)* Ah! *Mum!* Mum it's Claire. I've got the Police here. Can you and Dad come over? Something's happened to Adrian... No, please, I'll tell you when you get here... Bye. *(She puts down phone.)* They'll be here soon. It's not far.

CAMPBELL: Right. Then I think we'll get on. *(rises but does not take gloves)* There's lots to do...

WPC: Should I stay with Mrs Thorpe?

CLAIRE: No! I'll be fine. I'll have to phone the office.

CAMPBELL: I think Mrs Thorpe will be all right for a few minutes Rosie. We've got plenty to get on with. *(he moves to door)* Bye, Mrs Thorpe. You'll be here, presumably, if we need you for anything?

CLAIRE: Yes. Yes, of course. Goodbye Sergeant - and thanks for the tea. *(Rosie smiles uncertainly and follows Campbell out. We hear the outer door open and close. Claire rises and crosses to window, and watches carefully as they leave. She then turns)* Yes! I never thought - I should have realised. All those drug addicts, and drunkards. They were bound to - I bet you just waltzed in among them waving your wallet, Adrian. Just like the stupid trusting twit you were! Well it serves you right! *(looks at watch)* Come on Allan. We've got something to celebrate now. *(has idea)* Of course! That bottle of Bucks Fizz! I'll stick it in the fridge. *(she goes off)*

(Pause. Doorbell. She crosses doorway to answer door.) Is that you Mum? *(door opens)* Come in Mum. I thought you'd never get here. *(She enters, followed by ALLAN.)*

ALLAN: What's the "mum" business? Was that the Police I saw...

CLAIRE: Adrian's dead!

ALLAN: What?

CLAIRE: Burnt to death! In my car! Isn't it terrific?

(she hugs him)

ALLAN: Hang on a minute Claire. Tell me what's happened.

CLAIRE: He's done it! Well, he hasn't, but someone has.

ALLAN: Talk sense Claire, I can't...

CLAIRE: Adrian's body has been found in the burnt out remains of my car on some waste ground just off West Street.

ALLAN: But how did...?

CLAIRE: He took that bum back last night, like I told you, and the guy must have attacked him.

ALLAN: Are you sure about this?

CLAIRE: The Police are. They found the car - or what was left of it, and they found Adrian - or what was left of him. It couldn't have worked better if we'd planned it.

ALLAN: How do you know it was Adrian?

CLAIRE: Cufflinks! That old pair of cufflinks he got from his Dad. They were pretty blackened, but they survived the fire...

ALLAN: Are they sure it's him?

CLAIRE: Sergeant Campbell was. Awfully nice old man. Fussed over me. Got his WPC to make me a mug of tea. I nearly choked on it. Milk and sugar - he never even asked.

ALLAN: So the Police are happy it's Adrian in the car.

CLAIRE: Stop worrying! Now sit down, take your jacket off...

ALLAN: I should be at work - *(he takes off jacket and sits)* but we need to think this out.

CLAIRE: Later. I have a bottle of Bucks Fizz cooling in the fridge. *(She sits beside him and starts loosening his tie.)* I thought we should celebrate. Well, it's not every day my useless husband goes off and gets himself killed, leaving me a fortune. *(They kiss. ADRIAN appears from kitchen side of doorway. He is wearing the clothes Keith had on.)*

ADRIAN: *(as he enters)* Lo, tis the Phoenix, risen from - *(sees Allan)* What the hell is going on here?

CLAIRE: Adrian! What are you...

ALLAN: *(rising)* Am I glad to see you! We thought you had been killed...

ADRIAN: And you couldn't wait to get at it? *(he advances on Allan)* You're supposed to be a mate.

ALLAN: It's not like that Adrian! I was just - now just try to be calm...

ADRIAN: Sit down! Sit! *(Allan does)* No. Stand up. Go on. On your feet. I want to knock you down.

ALLAN: I think I'll just stay sitting.

ADRIAN: I might have known. *(turns)* And as for you...

CLAIRE: Adrian, I thought you were dead. The Police...

ADRIAN: I saw the Police. I waited for them to go. Then I made my way round the back and came in through the garden of the house behind us. I didn't realise you already had lover boy...

ALLAN: Now Adrian...

ADRIAN: Shut it! God, what a fool I've been! I've handed it to you on a plate, haven't I? I've killed myself off so that we could get this house off our backs and a nice little insurance pay out. So we could start afresh. And you - bitch - are going to get the lot! You had this all worked out from the start! There was no way I was going to get any of the money. *(he slumps in chair)*

(pause)

ALLAN: Perhaps I...

ADRIAN: Not another word Allan, or so help me I'll break your neck! *(pause)* I'm dead. I've set it up so that the Police think Keith killed me and burnt me in that fire. So how do I get the money now? Come on Adrian. Make it happen!

CLAIRE: We'll give you the money. We don't need it, do we Allan? Whatever's left after the house is paid off...

ADRIAN: Oh yes? You think I'm that daft? You two couldn't be trusted with the petty cash, never mind several thousand.

CLAIRE: You can have anything! *(she rises)*

ADRIAN: Where are you going?

CLAIRE: I need to go to the...

ADRIAN: You stay here. Any attempt to walk out that door, by either of you, and I'll kill you. I mean it! I'm in the mood, I can tell you. *(He gets drink.)* You thought I was too weak to kill Keith, because the thought of him burning alive was too much for me. Well, I showed you! It was different when he was out cold. *(He sits. Claire wanders to window)* I was driving round trying to find somewhere safe to stop. I was worried about going too close to one of the gathering places, in case they attacked me. Then I realised that was it! I could be attacked by Keith and the car set on fire! The Police must come up against that sort of thing. Idiot do-gooder goes down there all alone with smart car, money... So that's what I did. Parked the car, changed clothes with him, moved him into the driving seat, and set the car on fire. *(He is leaning forward intent on his story and Claire moves up behind his chair, with tie-back from curtains.)* It went up like something in the movies. Whoosh!

(Claire uses cord to strangle Adrian from behind.)

CLAIRE: Help me Allan! Help me! *(She struggles to hold Adrian. Allan crosses and holds him and they stand over him until he subsides. Pause.)*

ALLAN: *(checking)* He's dead!

CLAIRE: Of course he's dead! That was the idea!

ALLAN: But Claire...

CLAIRE: He'd have killed us. Can't you see that?

ALLAN: Maybe you're right. I don't know. This is all happening too fast. What are we going to do?

CLAIRE: All we have to do is to get rid of this body and everything's back as it was. We'll need to bury him somewhere.

ALLAN: Ok, Ok. What's done is done. But we can't bury him. It's all too easy for someone's dog to stumble across the body, and even years later they can - the gravel pits! You know the gravel pits just out beyond Handley Cross?

CLAIRE: No.

ALLAN: Well, it doesn't matter. There's a very deep lake out there. I can get the car down to within a few yards. I'll need something to weigh him down.

CLAIRE: There are some weights in the garage. He was into pumping iron for a while, before he got more interested in the booze.

ALLAN: Right. I'll back the car up into the garage and we'll... *(the doorbell rings)* Who the hell is that?

CLAIRE: How should I know? *(she moves towards window)*

ALLAN: Don't touch the curtains! Pretend there's no one in. *(Bell rings again.)*

CLAIRE: It'll be my Mum and Dad.

(The door is pounded on.)

CAMPBELL: *(off)* Mrs Thorpe? Mrs Thorpe? Are you all right? It's the Police. DS Campbell. Mrs Thorpe?

BLACKOUT AND CURTAIN